The Blind Fiddler

A play

Marie Jones

Samuel French — London
www.samuelfrench-london.co.uk

This play was originally performed by Lane Theatre
Company as part of the Edinburgh Fringe Festival in
2004 with the following cast:

Carol Moore
Marty Maguire
Julia Dearden
Paddy Jenkins

Based on a one act play by Marie Jones
The Blind Fiddler Of Glenadauch
produced by Charabanc Theatre Company in 1990
with the following cast:

Sean Kearns
Carol Scanlan
Sheila McWade

COPYRIGHT INFORMATION

CHARACTERS

Kathleen Gormley, as a ten-year-old and in her
  forties

Four other actors, M2 F2, play the following:

Mary Gormley, in her thirties and in her sixties
Pat Gormley, in his late thirties and late sixties
Joe Gormley, as an eleven-year-old and in his late
  thirties
Bridie Finnegan, Mary's sister, in her late thirties
Brendan McCann, late forties
John Jo McCann, his son, early twenties
Old Liam Flynn, late seventies
A Priest ⎫
Maggie ⎬ pilgrims to Lough Derg
Harry ⎪
Brian ⎭
Johnny McAdoo ⎫ re-enacting the Johnny McAdoo
Waiter ⎭ story
Manager of the concert hall
Barman ⎫
Chrissie Hagan ⎬ in a Drumquin pub
Johnny ⎪
Manus ⎭

The action of the play takes place in various settings
in Northern Ireland

Time — the present and thirty years ago

Other plays by Marie Jones
published by Samuel French Ltd

Women on the Verge of HRT

ACT I

Lough Derg, Northern Ireland

The back wall of the set is a mottled greenish colour and has doors and windows (unseen when closed) set into it. One door leads offstage; another opens up to reveal the back of a pub bar, with bottles, glasses etc. There is a sliding hatchway beside the bar door, through which people can appear. Other windows or doors open on to a chandelier, a church window, some dancing puppets and memory images of a man — Pat — playing the fiddle and a girl — the young Kathleen — writing a letter. Concealed elsewhere is a doll

In front and to the L of this wall is a raised area with steps leading up to it; the door leading offstage is on this level. This is used for scenes set upstairs. In front of the bar doors, on a diagonal, is a rostrum that can represent a pub bar counter

DS *there are two curved rostra at seating height suggesting the prow of a boat pointing at the audience; two straight rostra suggest the sides of the boat*

When the play begins, all the doors and windows in the back wall are closed. The Lights suggest cold and wet conditions. Music plays; it should have a mystical spiritual feel and reflect the ancient aura of the Lough Derg

Five pilgrims, including the adult Kathleen and a priest, stand in the boat, going towards an island

Priest (*over the music*) I am a pilgrim ... We are all pilgrims, making our journey to a holy place — to pay penance — to atone — to suffer, so we can be cleansed ... My fellow pilgrims and me about to enter into the same ritual together — leaving the material world behind.
Pilgrim 1 Did you ever know a year here when it didn't rain?
Kathleen And with no shoes on.
Priest To go barefooted.
Pilgrim 1 And starve.
Priest And fast. (*Pause*) St. Patrick's Cave.

Pilgrim 2 A penitentiary.
Priest Station Island.
Pilgrim 2 Looks like Alcatraz.
Kathleen Lough Derg.
All Lough Derg.

During the following the rostra that made the boat are re-arranged to look like a circle of stones — the remains of dwellings on Lough Derg

Music plays under the following: "Hail, Glorious St Patrick"

The pilgrims remove their shoes and move round in a circle, moving their arms in and out as is the ritual, and praying, either with rosaries or saying the Lord's Prayer

Pilgrim (*played by the actor playing Pat*) I renounce the world, the flesh and the devil. I renounce the world, the flesh and the devil.

At the end of the song Kathleen breaks away from the others, who carry on circling. Kathleen kneels at the bed of St Bridget

Kathleen St Patrick, St Bridget, you'll have to forgive me, but I am freezing —I'm starvin' — and I just want to go home ... Maybe my Ma was right ... She said I didn't know what sacrifice was ... I'll never stick it.

One of the circling Pilgrims, an old man, Harry, passes Kathleen. He is having difficulty walking over the stones

Kathleen Do you want an arm, mister?
Old Man No, you're all right, I have walked over these stones for the past thirty years and I will do it myself until God calls me.

During the following the Lights fade on the pilgrims and they drift away and exit

We still hear the music and the mumbling of prayers

Kathleen Why did my father do this, St Bridget? Like that old man, every year for thirty years ... He never mentioned God, never went to Mass — and yet at seventy he was still walking bare-footed over these rocks ... Maybe he sat here and prayed for me — you probably know all about me — or maybe he never mentioned me at all ... Well, St Bridget, that's why I am here — for him — in his place — to try and understand why ... I suppose I never really knew him — never really knew why he gave ... Sitting here, in the cold and the rain, trying to get to know a dead person — trying to get close to a soul — a dead man — a spirit ... This is crazy ... All those years on this earth and I never knew him ... Why did he come here? Was it guilt? What did he pray for? And when he came home, that look on his face — he sparkled, his eyes were as bright as I'd ever seen them ... He changed ... I was jealous ... Why could I not do that for him? As a child I wanted to, but there was always — something that seemed to trouble him — deep down.

The Lights fade on Kathleen

The music changes; a fiddle plays

A window — the one behind which is the picture of Pat Gormley with the fiddle — opens and a Light comes up on it

The Lights come up in the pub and the bar door is opened to reveal the bottles and glasses. Glasses are set on the bar

The Pilgrims become Pat Gormley, a man in his forties, John Jo, and Brendan, John Jo's father, who has a fiddle. (If additional musicians are available they can be in the pub setting too)

Pat appears to be listening and looking to a room above

Kathleen, now a child, moves to the middle of the room, dancing. John Jo dances with her, and Brendan plays the fiddle

Pat (*trying to calm them down*) Keep it down, you'll have the peelers in on us.

They ignore him

Will ye keep her quiet, lads ... I think I hear footsteps above.

They ignore him

Mary, Kathleen's mother, enters in her dressing gown and bangs a bottle of bleach on the table

Mary What the hell is going on here? What is going on? Right you lot, out ... Luk at the time, you're full drunk.

Brendan Sorry, Mary ... We just got carried away ... My Uncle Petey got buried the day ... You know how it is — just givin' him a wee send-off.

Mary Any excuse.

John Jo Not an excuse, the man is dead — a goner — swear ... I seen them put him in the hole — right, Da?

Brendan Oh, he's well dead, all right.

Mary He would have to be to put up with that racket.

John Jo Sure, no harm, Mary.

Mary No harm? Harm to ones that has to listen to it ... (*Turning to Pat*) Harm all right if the peelers hear that carry on ... Next thing you know the Rebel songs start.

Pat I told them to keep it down, but they wouldn't listen.

Mary You're too soft. They'll listen to me ... Right John Jo McCann, out — my two children have to get up for school in the morning.

John Jo Sure your Kathleen is ——

Pat (*giving John Jo a look*) Come on, John Jo, get your Da home.

Mary My Kathleen is what?

Brendan She is a great youngster and very smart.

Pat John Jo.

Mary And her brother is smarter, cos he has the wit not to sneak down here when he should be doing his homework ... (*To Pat*) Hope our Kathleen wasn't down here the night.

John Jo No ... I never seen her ... We never seen her, sure we didn't, Da.

Mary Pat.

Pat Earlier on — she was doing her sums with me.

Brendan (*parcelling up his fiddle*) Going now, Mary — (*to John Jo*) 'mon, son.

Mary You have bin told — no music in this pub — and don't bring that yoke back in here — you will get us arrested.

Brendan I know, its just oul Petey … We had to have a wee halfin for Petey ... You have to make allowances for the dead, Mary.

Mary And what about making allowances for the livin'?

Brendan We got carried away …

Mary Well, if you don't bring that thing in, you will have no call to get carried away … and what kind of an example are ye showin' til your son?

Brendan A brave one I'll have ye know, for he is near as good as me on this …

Mary Well, I must say, that is going to get him far ... Working yet, John Jo?

John Jo Getting the odd wee turn at the roofin' Mary, and sure, there's always England ... A couple of mates....

Brendan You're not going to that heathen place.

Mary Just hurry up and get out ... This was meant to be my night off, you know.

Brendan (*sticking the fiddle up his coat*) Come on, John Jo ... Sorry Mary. (*He makes a face behind her back*) Oiche maith, Pat.

Mary And none of that oul talk either — it's dangerous.

Brendan Jais' sake, it's like going for a drink in the library ... Goodnight.

Pat I'll show you out.

Brendan and John Jo leave (with the additional musicians)

Mary starts to clear the glasses

Pat You go on up love, I'll do that.

Mary Can't be leavin' it til the morning, I don't want to come down to a stench of stale drink and tobacco.

Pat I'm sorry, love, it won't happen again.

Mary You said that the last time. Pat ... Can't you see that I'm scared? If we lose the Protestant customers we may close this pub. You heard what the Prime Minister said?

Pat What, if you treat Catholics like Protestants they'll behave like them?

Mary O'Neil is trying to be fair to us all.

Pat Do you think that's fair?

Mary Yes. That's why you don't want to throw all that Rebel stuff in their faces.

Pat I know, Mary ... Sorry ... The coast was clear, we checked outside. Nobody heard a thing and with Brendan's uncle Peter being a country man ... It's the custom.

Mary There cud be peelers about, even people passin'. You don't know who you can trust these days ... I don't want it to happen ever again ... Pat, do you hear me?

Pat Yes ... Don't worry.

Mary I don't want our children woken in the night by a lot of ould drunks, singing and cavortin'.

Pat It won't happen again.

Mary Protestant people don't want that thrown in their faces.

Pat Mary, I heard you, just go on up.

Mary Someday I will get my children out of that pigeon loft.

Mary exits

Kathleen That was close, Daddy.

Pat You are going to get me into terrible trouble, our Kathleen … She spied Chrissie Hagan there. Give her a minute and then you sneak up ...

Kathleen Chrissie says can she have the dregs out of the glasses for she has a drouth on her …

Pat And quit that oul talk or your mother will have me hung.

Pat starts to clear up and Kathleen follows him around the bar

Kathleen Why is m' mammy scared — sure it's only singin'.

Pat Your mammy is right, some customers wouldn't like it.

Kathleen She said Protestant customers.

Pat Up you go … Go on.

Kathleen What did she mean?

Pat Have you done your sums the night?

Kathleen Yes.

Pat Five multiplied by nine.

Kathleen Forty-two.

Pat Forty-five.

Kathleen What did she mean … Why is she scared?

Pat This is a mixed pub, you have to keep everybody happy.

Kathleen Do Protestants not like singing?

Pat Course they do.

Kathleen Then what was she talking about?

Pat Nine eights.

Kathleen Seventy-six.

Pat Seventy-two.

Kathleen I love it down here, Daddy … Brendan and John Jo are a geg.

Pat Not one word to your mother, promise me.

Kathleen Promise.

Pat Our secret.

Kathleen Our secret. Cross my heart and hope to die.

Pat Seven eights.

Kathleen Fifty-six.

Pat Great ... Now scram. (*He sings "Champion the Wonderhorse"*)

Bridie enters. She is Mary's sister, in her thirties, a bit tipsy. She carries a whiskey glass

Bridie Where is everybody?

Kathleen Aunt Bridie.

Pat Bridie, what the hell are you doing here? Do ya know the time?

Bridie I was sittin' in the snug there. Put a wee whiskey in that, Pat. Sure, I never heard last orders — I'm only in.

Kathleen Aunt Bridie, you have been in since half seven, for I seen ye comin' in.

Bridie I didn't know ye had Dixon a Dock Green working for ye ... All right, I fell asleep your honour ... (*Of her glass*) A wee halfin, Pat.

Pat I'll have the peelers in on me.

Bridie Peelers, me arse ... I am family.

Pat (*giving her the drink*) Make it quick, Bridie ... I need to close up.

Kathleen Aunt Bridie, can I come to the markets some day with you and help you sell your regs?

Bridie Regs, what are you on about? It's good clothes I sell — good clothes that come from the Antrim Road.

Kathleen My mammy says they are regs.

Bridie Oh, your ma thinks she is a bloody lady ... There was fifteen of us and all our ma cud afford to put on our backs was regs — now b'god she thinks she is a cut above the rest.

Kathleen She says she is going to get us out of here to a nice house, with a better class of people.

Bridie (*drinking her drink*) Oh, aye, and she thinks a better class of people is not going to luk down their noses at her, like she luks down on us.

Pat She just wants to get on, Bridie, no harm in that ... Kathleen, this is the last time — go — now.

Kathleen Don't worry, Aunt Bridie, I'm not going to a better class of people — I am going to stay here with all youse, in the pub ... Night night.

Bridie And remember it's rags not regs ...

Pat Six nines.

Kathleen Am .... fifty-six.

Pat is about to correct her

Bridie (*impressed*) Oh, a wee smartarse are ye as well.

Kathleen My mammy says our Joe is dead smart and he is gonna go to grammar school.

Bridie I declare to God I have never seen that brother of yours with a dirty face, not natural that.

Kathleen I have a dirty face all the time — me and Chrissie.

Bridie Nothin' wrong with a good bit of honest dirt, you tell your ma that.

Kathleen My mammy is always cleaning.

Bridie Ay, if she's not careful , she'll clean herself intil a Protestant.

Kathleen What do ya mean, Bridie?
Pat Kathleen, now, or that is the last I'll let you in here.
Kathleen Night-night, Aunt Bridie.
Bridie Night-night, love.

Pat smiles

Pat (*whispering the right answer into Kathleen's ear*) Fifty-four.

Kathleen exits

Bridie You're a dacent man, Pat Gormley, cos you don't forget who you are and where you come from.
Pat Time to go, Bridie.
Bridie Our Mary was born and reared like me here in the Markets. I don't forget who I am … Once ya do, you're nothing ... God bless ye, Pat.
Pat God bless ya, Bridie.

Bridie exits; Pat is left alone

The Lough Derg music plays and the Lights change to the Lough Derg setting. The pub door is closed

Pat exits

The adult Kathleen enters and kneels. She says three Hail Marys

Kathleen My mother knew all about sacrifice, St Patrick ... This would have been easy for her ... She sacrificed to get what she wanted — and he went along — he said nothing ... They shared each other's dreams at one time — Pat's Pub — but it wasn't enough ... She wanted us kids out — away from all the stupid drunken fools ... He didn't fight for us ... He knew it would be another life, he knew he couldn't give us the things that meant something to him … I wanted to know about him and his stories and his music, he desperately wanted me to know … Joe didn't give a damn and yet my da gave … Why Da … Why I could make that troubled look on your face disappear, it was me, wasn't it, Da?

The Lights cross-fade to the uper level, Kathleen's bedroom

Kathleen produces a doll and lies down on the upper level, holding the doll, watching and waiting

Pat enters

Pat Kathleen. Kathleen. It's way past your bedtime. Come on. Now tell
me, what story does Chrissie Hagan want tonight?

Kathleen She wants the one about when you were a wee buck in
Drumquin.

Pat Which one, sure there's hundreds.

Kathleen The one about the man and his mates that ate all the grub …

Pat Oh, you mean Johnny McAdoo?

Kathleen Daddy, is that a true story?

Pat Would I tell you a word of a lie?

Kathleen No … I don't think so.

Pat Well, if you don't believe me, I'm not going to be telling you.

Kathleen I do — I definitely do.

Pat Well. (*As if telling a story*) Johnny McAdoo and me and McFee and
another two or three went on a spree one day, well we had a bob or
two which we knew how to blew, and the beer and whiskey flew and
we all felt gay.

During the following a separate area of light comes up

*Two of the actors enter the new light area and perform the roles of
Johnny McAdoo and the waiter, re-enacting the story Pat tells*

Music starts

(*Singing to Kathleen*) We visited McCann's, MacLamann's,
Humpty Dan's,
We then went into Swann's, our stomachs for to pack.
We ordered a feed which indeed we did need,
And we finished it with speed but we still felt slack.

Johnny McAdoo turned red, white and blue,
And a plate of Irish stew he soon put out of sight.
He shouted out "encore", with a roar, for some more,
That he'd never felt before such a keen appetite.

He ordered eggs and ham, bread and jam, what a cram,
But him we couldn't ram though we tried our level best.
For everything we bought, cold or hot, mattered not,
It went down him like a shot and he still stood the test.

He swallowed tripe and lard, by the yard, we got scared,
We thought it'd go hard when the waiter brought the bill.
We told him to give o'er but he swore he could lower
Twice as much again and more before he had his fill.

He nearly sucked a trough full of broth; said McGrath,
"He'll devour the tablecloth if you don't hold him in."
When the waiter brought the charge, McAdoo felt so large,
He began to scold and barge and his blood went on fire.
He began to curse and swear, tear his hair, in despair,
And to finish the affair, called the shopman a liar.

The shopman he drew out, and no doubt, he did clout,
McAdoo he kicked about like an old football.
He tattered all his clothes, broke his nose, I suppose,
He would've killed him with a few blows in no time at all.

McAdoo began to howl and to growl, by my soul,
He threw an empty bowl at the shopkeeper's head.
It struck by Mickey Flynn, peeled the skin off his chin,
And the ructions did begin and we all fought and bled.

The peelers did arrive, man alive, four or five,
At us began to drive for us all to march away.
We paid for all the meat that we ate, stood a treat,
And went home to ruminate on the spree that day.

(*Speaking*) Good-night darling.

*The Lights go down on Kathleen and up on the pub. The pub door is
opened*

   Johnny McAdoo and the waiter exit

   *Mary enters, takes a bottle of sherry and a glass from the shelf behind
   the door, and sits*

Pat returns to the pub

Mary Do you want a wee sherry?
Pat No, I see enough of drink, love.
Mary Come and sit down a minute, Pat.
Pat Sit down?
Mary It's all right — there's only a couple in the snug and they're
   served.
Pat (*sitting*) What's up?

Mary I have seen a house up the Cave Hill Road ... It's lovely, three bedrooms, a big garden — a living room downstairs, like normal people.

Pat So you're serious.

Mary (*pouring herself a drink*) What do you think, love?

Pat I think. We can't afford it.

Mary I have it worked out ——

Pat And how do you do that?

Mary We have the pub paid out, we can borrow against it ...

Pat Mary, we've only just stopped borrowing.

Mary The business is good — and we can let the rooms out upstairs for lodgin's which will pay the mortgage on the new house.

Pat Lodgin's.

Mary I'll take less housekeeping ... You know how good I am at making do.

Pat I never heard the kids complaining or wanting us to move.

Mary They are young, they are not lookin' to the future, that is for us to do for them.

Pat We'll talk about it again ...

Mary I want to talk about it now.

Pat (*getting up and tidying the bar counter*) No, and you're running out of Vim for the toilets.

Mary Why are you doing this to me?

Pat (*stopping*) What, Mary, am I doing to you?

Mary Making it hard — that's what you are doing.

Pat Oh, I am sorry ... You are about to take my two kids away from their home, knowing full well I will hardly see them, or you ... but God forbid I should make it hard for you, Mary.

The hatch opens and Brendan looks through

Brendan Hey, Pat, give us two wee Willies and a halfin for Bridie.

Pat Right.

Brendan disappears. Pat puts the drinks on the bar counter

Mary (*closing the hatch*) Pat, please try and understand ... Why are you fighting me? We can't sit by and watch the children try and grow up surrounded by drink and foul language and no-hopers ... We are Catholics ... They have to do well ... They are going to get no favours in this city if they don't.

Pat It was your idea to get this pub.

Mary Yes, as a way of having the means to do for our kids what we never had.

Pat And our wee Kathleen loves it. Our Joe is a bright wee buck, it has done him no harm … They have all your family here — they are good people, Mary.

Mary Good people, good people that have nothing to show for it.

Pat What do you want them to show for being good decent people? Is being good and decent not enough for you?

Mary No it's not, cos it's not for me it's for our Kathleen and our Joe … My family are all good people ...

The hatch opens and John Jo looks through

John Jo Hey, Pat — is Mary givin' you earache?

Mary Mind your own, John Jo.

Brendan pops his head through

Brendan His ma gives me earache, morning noon and night … Thank god for pubs, eh, son?

Mary slides the hatch door closed

Pat Mary, could we please just keep this until closing.

Mary I want my kids educated. Now the first black mark in their copybook is living above this pub. What way will they end up? Look at our Joe, he is that smart he would near scare you ... The teacher says he is brilliant at piano … Our Joe, playing the piano in a place like this — he would be laughed at.

Pat Mary, you know I'll hardly see them ... I will be home at all hours and they'll be in bed — at least here, I can see them after school, at dinner time, and put them to bed and tell them stories, just what my da did for us.

Mary Pat, I know you love to live in all that past — but you fill our Kathleen's head with stories about drunken farmers and how wonderful things were in your day in the country, she thinks it some fairytale place where life was one big round of reels and jigs ... I caught her the other day mashing up potatoes, telling her doll she was makin' her poteen.

Pat She is a right wee case.

Mary It's not funny: truth is, you were poor, you were given nothin' to start you out in life ... This is a city, Pat — a big city and our children have to make their way in it — and they will, if it kills me.

Pat Mary, what happened to the carefree wee girl I married?

Mary Different times now, Pat.

Pat The times don't change what's in people's heart.

Mary I don't forget the struggle we had to get this place, but we did it together, you and me. I know you didn't want to give up that land your da left, you wanted to keep a part of you there in Drumquin … We would have got nowhere in this life with a couple of oul fields and you give them up, sold them for us, for this — it made sense.

Pat Now, you are asking me to give up my children and you, that does not make sense Mary.

Mary Pat, you are not giving us up … I'll still be your wife, they'll still be your children … You are providing for them … What more can a father do for his children?

Pat I can give them time, Mary, I want them to know who I am, where I came from, what matters to me … If we move, I'm frightened it will drive them away from me, make them ashamed of who they are, where they are from.

Mary It's a sacrifice worth makin'.

Pat What is making you so hard?

Mary I'm not being hard. I look round me, I see no future for them. I see them as us.

Pat We had a future Mary, we made a future … We have this.

Mary And at what cost? Scrimpin', savin', working our fingers to the bones.

Pat But, Mary, you don't understand. We never lost each other in all of that. The price for their future could be something we can't buy back, we can't get a mortage on or sell something for … Are you willing to pay that?

Mary is silent. She can say nothing

Mary Pat — we will still love you. Pat?

Pat Ah, no, Mary …

Pat doesn't want to continue the conversation; he opens the hatch

Brendan and John Jo appear in the hatchway

Pat John Jo.

John Jo Pat.

Pat John Jo.

John Jo We're just talking about oul Liam there.

Mary exits

Pat Oh yeah, how's he doing?

John Jo The priest is with him now … Hasn't long.

Brendan   We have a wee favour to ask ye, Pat.

Pat   Oh ay. Fire away …

John Jo Y' know the way oul Liam is in the nursin' home and know the way his wife won't let him come home to his own home, dead or alive?

Pat   That's a bit hard, and him about to die.

Brendan   That's cos he had already left her for an oul one in the nursing home.

John Jo But he shouldn't a told the wife, cos there was no way she was goin' to find out, for neither him nor the oul one he touched for could get up out of their chairs anyway — but oul Liam had to blurt it out to the wife.

Brendan   So, the wife has tould him, when he dies he can do whatever the hell he likes but he's not comin' home til her … Stupid ghett shud a kept his trap shut.

Pat   Tell me boys, where do I fit intil all this?

John Jo Well, oul Bridie was thinkin'— so she was …

Pat   What — what was Bridie thinkin'?

John Jo Ack, just … You know the way Bridie thinks now and again.

Pat   Yes and …?

Bridie pops her head up in the hatchway

Bridie   I knew youse two big yellow balloons hadn't the nerve on yis to ask ... Pat, it's our Mary's night of a Tuesday to stay with m'ma ... Could we have a wee wake for Liam, for he shud definitely be dead by Tuesday — well, according to the word on the streets.

Pat   You know what Mary is like, Bridie — she wud hit the roof — my life wud not be worth livin'.

Bridie   She won't be here, she won't know.

Brendan   He was from round about your neck a the woods, too ... he was a Tyrone man, way back.

Bridie   Ah, lave it lads, for our Mary has him ruled.

Pat thinks for a moment; they all watch and wait

Brendan   Desperate the poor man has to die without a proper send off for his soul.

Pat   You know what, lads, you're right, yes, the man deserves what is rightly due to him.

Bridie   Stikin' out. I am going to speak to the sister up at the home, see if we can get the coffin round here for an hour.

Pat The coffin!

Bridie How would you like to be waked and not be there?

Pat Bridie, we can wake the man's spirit but I don't know about the coffin …

Brendan Not the same, Pat.

Pat You can bring your instruments, well hid now … Don't be telling everybody and no big crowds — and no coffin.

John Jo Hey Da, we could get uncle Paddy to bring it over in the coal lorry and then take it back.

Pat I said we'll wake the man's spirit but no coffin …That's seven and sixpence.

Brendan Eh?

The Lights fade. The Lough Derg music plays. The pub door is closed

The basilica. The door in the back wall concealing the church window is opened; light, as if from a church, streams through it. The sounds of music, singing and praying as if from a chapel come up and continue under the following scene

The adult Kathleen enters as if from the basilica and walks as if to the water's edge. She bathes her feet

Maggie, a woman around the same age, comes out and joins Kathleen

Maggie Hard to stay awake.

Kathleen Stick your feet in the water, that'll wake you up.

Maggie I am starving.

Kathleen I thought it was only me. Everybody just seems so into it — your heart scared to say you're starvin' in case you get deported.

Maggie No point in comin' here if you don't stick to the fast ... Maggie Martin ...

Kathleen Kathleen Mullen ...

Maggie Any fags?

Kathleen Are you allowed to smoke?

Maggie You're smoking it, not eating it. (*She puts her feet in the water*) Jesus, that water's cold … Look at this place, middle a summer and you can see nothing for the mist … Eerie ... S'pose if the weather was good here you wouldn't feel you suffered enough ... They say God does that. You have to suffer so we can be cleansed ... You'd better believe it ...

Kathleen Have you been before?

Maggie Every year for the last ten years, wouldn't miss it.

There is a pause; they listen to the singing coming from the chapel

Listen … Beautiful, isn't it? It's a wonder the bloody place doesn't sink with the weight of Catholic guilt.

Kathleen When it's over, after the three days, are you rid of it?

Maggie I'm not guilty ... I'm not even religious ... I don't believe in God ...

Kathleen Then why are you here?

Maggie For myself ... I like all the ritual and the praying and the singing ... The constant dronin' on and on and on … Takes you out of yourself … You get caught up in it.

Kathleen I haven't … My father came here every year — I never knew why. He died just this year and I want to try and understand.

Maggie A bit late, do you not think?

Kathleen I don't think so — not if I knew why he came, what he wanted.

Maggie Everybody has their own reasons … Tell ye what, a shrink would have a field day here — plenty of troubled souls — more baggage on this island than there is in Heathrow Airport.

Kathleen Maybe it was a way for him to just — get away from the world — from us, from her, maybe he was just selfish, and that's it, nothing more to it than that …

Maggie Stop thinking about him, think about you — then it might work.

Kathleen It's hard being angry with a dead person … What do you do? Can't dig them up.

Maggie Just imagine they're here; sometimes it's not about what they need to say to you to stop you being angry, it's what you need to say to them … Do you know what the next station is?

Kathleen No.

Maggie Kneel at the entrance to St. Patrick's bed, say three Our Fathers, three Hail Marys, and one creed. Walk three times round the inside while repeating prayers. Kneel at the Cross in the centre and say them again — and when you have finished that I'll meet ye back here for our daily ration of Lough Derg soup.

Kathleen I look forward to that.

Maggie You haven't tasted it yet ... Cheers.

Maggie exits

Kathleen He must have wanted for us what she wanted — yet he always used to say, you can give them all the education in the world — but what about their souls, Mary — but what about what is in here ... We never knew what he meant and she would look at him like he was talking a foreign language and say — what's in here (*pointing to her head*) is what matters ... If he never wanted the Cave Hill Road, why did he let her have her way, he just accepted it ... There could have been a way — a compromise, but she was too scared — like a little scared bird that flew to the top branch of a very tall tree too frightened to look down — just relieved that it managed to get there at all.

The Lights change to an outdoor setting. Music plays, the piano being the dominant sound

The church window is concealed. One of the rostra is moved R *to become a bench*

Joe, as a young boy, runs on and stops as if arriving at the top of a hill. He stands, not too close to the edge, a bit frightened to go to the edge. He looks for a stone, finds one, gets on his belly, looks over the edge and throws the stone

Joe (*shouting*) Mammy I'm first ... I'm here.
Mary Be careful.
Joe Mammy, I'm right on the edge.

Mary enters carrying a picnic basket

Mary Come you away from there, our Joe ... Come on, get back, it's dangerous.

Joe slides back on his tummy and gets up and looks out

Joe Where is it, Mammy? You said we would be able to see it from here.
Mary Wait for our Kathleen; I want us all to see it together.
Joe (*shouting down the hill*) Hurry up, you.
Mary Always an oul slowcoach our Kathleen. (*She sets the picnic rug down and the basket and begins to set food out on the rug*)
Joe Mammy, can I have the biggest slice of the queen cake?
Mary Ay son, before our Kathleen gets to it for she wud ate the arm of ye — greedy gorb.
Joe Will we really have a piano in it, Mammy?
Mary We will, son, I don't care if I don't have a chair to sit on as long as you have a piano. Mrs Munroe says you have the makings of a great

piano player — she says you could some day play in an orchestra if
you keep up the practising.

Joe An orchestra.

Mary (*shouting*) Kathleen, what the hell is keepin' ye?

Kathleen (*off*) I'm comin'.

Mary Playing in big places with chandeliers and all ... Ya know,
like, what's yer man's name? Him on the TV of a Sunday night ...
Mantovani.

Joe Chandeliers? What are chandeliers?.

Mary Big lights with big diamonds drippin' from them.

Kathleen enters, puffed and carrying a bunch of flowers

Kathleen I am flippin' sweatin'.

Joe I'm not.

Kathleen Who cares?

Mary It's about time.

Kathleen (*handing Mary the flowers*) Here, Mammy ... I picked them.

Mary Ack, thanks, love, they're lovely. (*She stands and puts the
flowers on the bench*) Now, come on ... Stand over here, the both of
yis. Kathleen ... just here.

Joe and Kathleen stand by Mary

Now look way down there... You see where that red post van is
turning? Down that street with all the trees, that's where we will be
moving — right there on the Cave Hill Road. Say it — altogether
— after three ... one, two three ...

All The Cave Hill Road.

Mary Beautiful, isn't it? Your address won't be above a pub any more
it will be — let me hear it.

Joe The Cave Hill Road. Will the big fellas on the Cave Hill Road hit
me, Mammy? The ones round the markets do.

Kathleen That's cos you're a big cissy, our Joe, they touch me and I
dig their heads in.

Joe Ay, and then they go and get about ten of their brothers.

Mary No, that won't happen up the Cave Hill Road — won't be no big
families, mostly Protestants and a better class of Catholic — and you
won't have no oul drunk men singing out your front window.

Kathleen Mammy.

Mary What?

Kathleen picks up the flowers from the bench and hands them to Mary

Kathleen Can I pour the lemonade?

Mary No, you cannot, for you're that clumsy you'll spill it ... I'll do it.
(*She hands Joe the biggest piece of cake*)

Joe Look Kathleen, I got the biggest bit.

Kathleen That's not fair.

Mary It is, he's a boy ... Here, there's yours. (*She offers Kathleen a piece*)

Kathleen I don't want it.

Mary sighs contentedly

Mary (*singing to herself*) I am Mary from the Cave Hill Road,
               Mary from the Cave Hill Road.
               I'll have a garden and a gate ——
     (*She thinks of the next line*)
               — And I'll stay at home and bake
               I'm Mary from the Cave Hill Road.
(*Walking over to the edge and looking over; speaking*) Smell the grass
and the trees and all ... That's the smell we are going to wake up to
every morning — no more stale drink and tobacco — grass, fresh
cut, cos I will be out every morning mowing it — I will have it like
a billiard table — lovely smooth green grass on the Cave Hill Road
— primroses in the garden ... Nice people passin' my front door ...
"Good morning, Mrs Gormley," they'll say, "and how are you and
how are the children?" ... "Oh, good morning Mrs — am — Hamilton
... Joe's playing the piano now you know, would you like to come in
for a cup of coffee? A cup of coffee (*she laughs at the idea*) and a
currant square. I have just baked them ... Oh, would you like to say
hallo to my children ... This is Joe —Joe say good-morning to Mrs ...
Hamilton."

Joe (*embarrassed*) Mammy.

Mary He's a bit shy ... Come on, Joe.

Joe Mornin' Missis.

Mary Ing ... ing ... morning ... You must use your "ings" Joe.

Joe Morning, Mrs Hamilton.

Mary My daughter Kathleen.

Kathleen I want to stay with my daddy in the pub.

Mary (*angry that Kathleen has barged into her imagination*) Well, you
can't, you will have to settle down our Kathleen. Our Joe is going to
grammar school and if you don't knuckle down you will end up in
secondary ... Luk at the state of ye, covered in crumbs.

Kathleen I'm going to miss Teresa and Francine and Josie and
everybody, I won't have no friends on the Cave Hill Road.

Joe You will meet new friends — better than the riff-raff you play with.
They all say f. u. c. k., don't they, mammy?

Kathleen Then you come from riff-raff, Mammy, cos that's where you were born.

Joe They are all dunces so they are, half of them never even went to big school.

Mary Shut up both of yis.

Kathleen Doesn't matter, my daddy left school at thirteen and he is dead clever.

Joe (*laughing*) Dead clever? Sure he doesn't even know how to do decimals, sure he doesn't, Mammy.

Kathleen So — he is a good barman and everybody loves him.

Mary Our Kathleen, you would start a row in an empty house.

Joe His friends are all oul smelly drunks.

Mary Don't worry, you won't be seeing much more of them smelly drunks.

Kathleen That's m'Aunt Bridie your talking about, and if she's smelly, then so are you Mammy, cos she is your sister.

Joe Mammy says Bridie is as common as muck.

Kathleen Bridie calls Mammy an uppety oul hure. I heard her.

Mary Right we are going home. (*She packs the picnic up during the following*)

Joe We are only here.

Mary Don't care, I can't take yis anywhere I have to listen to yis carpin. I have had enough.

Joe Mammy says Bridie is a dirty oul tart cos she sucks up to men.

Mary Stop that bad talk.

Kathleen I am going to kick your bollicks in, our Joe.

Mary (*losing it*) Jesus Christ, the sooner I get youse two away from them foulmouth hures a bloody hell the better.

Joe (*shocked*) Ah ah ah! You said bad words.

Mary Any the two of youse friggers opens your mouth again you'll get my fist down it —now lift that rug and come on — ungrateful wee ghetts.

Kathleen (*to Joe*) And don't make fun of our daddy ever again ... At least he can play the fiddle and sing cos I've heard him.

Mary (*stopping dead*) What ... You go now ... What did you say?

Kathleen Nothin'.

Mary Play the fiddle and sing … Play the bloody fiddle and bloody sing ... Where did you hear this, when did you hear this?

Kathleen Nowhere, I was only jokin'.

Mary (*slapping Kathleen*) Where? Tell me where.

Kathleen I'm not supposed to say.

Mary (*slapping Kathleen again*) Where? Tell me where.

Kathleen I'm not supposed to say — don't make me tell you, please.

The Lights cross-fade to the bar and the door is opened. A crate of empty bottles is set

Mary and Joe leave

Kathleen is in the bar. She goes to the hatch and opens it

Brendan puts his head in through the hatchway

Kathleen Coast clear, daddy?
Pat (*off* L) Coast clear, Kathleen.
Kathleen Coast clear, Brendan.
Brendan Coast clear. I'll stay by the front door for a while and keep dick.

Brendan exits R

Kathleen Tell John Jo he can bring Liam in now.

Pat enters

Kathleen Daddy, is Mammy definitely left?
Pat Definitely left, love. (*He gestures to Kathleen to take the crate of empties away*)

Kathleen leaves with the crate

John Jo and Bridie wheel in oul Liam in a coffin

Pat is speechless for a moment

Pat Jesus Christ.
Liam I'm still here, Pat.
Bridie The oul bugger didn't die.
Liam I wanna be the first man to be alive at his own wake.
Pat You toul me he died.
John Jo I know, but sure if I had toul you he was still alive you wud a told me to wait until he did die, and isn't it better we have him here … Sure luk at him, he is near as dead that makes no difference, isn't that right, Liam?
Liam I am, I sware, the priest said as much ... I just pulled through at the last, but I cud go soon enough.
Pat Yis, tuk the bloody mickey out of me.

Bridie We couldn't take the chance of our Mary being here — so we just says to ourselves, dead or alive we will stick to the Tuesday.

Liam You're a brave man, Pat Gormley; many's another publican wud be scared to do what you're doin' ... It's terrible times when a fiddle can put the fear a God into people —even when it's a man's right.

Pat (*giving in*) Well ...

They all wait in anticipation to hear what he has to say

When it's a man's right, what can you do?

John Jo Good man yerself, Pat ... Dixie Devlin had a few boys upstairs of his pub last week having a few tunes and the peelers raided — said Dixie was recruiting for the IRA — did ye ever.

Kathleen enters

Kathleen (*looking at them all*) Liam.

Liam Jesus, young Kathleen, you're fairly growed.

Kathleen You're not dead.

Liam I likely will be, next week ... Another wee Bushmills there, Pat.

Kathleen But how can you have a wake if he's not dead?

Bridie Stop you complicating things, Miss Knowitall — I'll take my usual.

Pat pours the drinks during the following

Liam Ay, children the day are far too smart for their own good.

Kathleen What's the point of having a party … ?

Bridie No time for thinking; the matron says he has to be back in an hour.

Liam An hour for a wake — desperate.

Bridie Stop gurnin', you're lucky you're gettin' one.

John Jo Now Liam, seeing as you are at your own wake, what is your pleasure?

Liam Well, ya see, me and that man Gormley there, we grew up in the same neck a the woods in Drumquin — and a story that was passed on to me I am sure was passed on til Pat there — it's the story of the Blind Fiddler of Glenadauch when he come to the town. Tell us when he came to your house.

Kathleen Yes, Daddy, please tell us.

Bridie Right, Pat, will we give it a lash for oul Liam.

Pat We will so.

John Jo Aye Maith thu Maith thu.

The following is enacted by everybody, with music

Pat Well, when we were all young bucks —there was the seven of us — and me mother toul us one night as she set by the fire: "Times is desperate hard for your da, childer; the crops is poorly and I don't know how I'm gonna feed yis at all." And suddenly there was a fierce knock on the door. Now our wee Johnny, who was only two hands higher than a poe, climbs up til the windy ... He cud hardly get the words out for the excitement: "It's the Blind Fiddler."

Kathleen The Blind Fiddler from Glenadauch — the Blind Fiddler has come for to play for us.

Pat And my mother, God have mercy on her, got intil a holy state ...

Bridie Oh sweet Jesus, it's the Blind Fiddler and me not a bite in the cupboard ...

Pat You haft for to feed and water the Blind Fiddler.

Liam It's bad luck if ye don't.

Pat "Let the Man in", says our Manus.

John Jo Let the man in.

Pat He being the cut of a giant but as supersticious as they come — so in he comes ...

Liam God bless all here.

Pat "And God Bless you, sir", we all pipes up.

All And God bless you, sir.

Pat And our wee Johnny, not a bit bother on him — goes over to the fiddler, takes him by the hand and leads him over til the chair by the fire. The fiddler had no sooner struck the fiddle w'his bow when there was another fierce knock on the door. In came ould bent over Seammie McGinn with his squeeze box to play with the Blind Fiddler. He went over beside the fiddler and plunked himself down and futered about on the squeeze box until he found the fiddler's key. Good man yourself. Seamie wheezed for he had been blighted with the asthma … Then in packles Chrissie Hagan who was always with, and I mean always with, child, but was a quare turn at the liltin' — she gives oul Seamie a big dunt and knocks him flyin across the room, intil the sofa, and shouts "Give us an oul jig, fiddler". "They're all comin' up the lane, Mammy, with their instruments." "Jesus," says my mammy and she whispers into our Manus's big ear, "For they will be all lukin' fed too."

John Jo Contain yourself, Mammy, and say a prayer for it's the custom, and we can't worry about grub for the time being.

Pat He whispers back ... Well, in they all come, led by wee Jamsie McAleer, weighted down with God knows how many bottles of poteen. "Take a sup," says he, "for isn't this some of the best poteen you will get this side of Tyrone." So we supped — and we supped —

and we supped — and even the weeins were at it and them hid under
the big table for fear m'mammy would see them. And we danced —
and we jigged — and we supped, and one thing and another until the
scrake of dawn. M'mammy had forgot all about the empty cupboard.
And then, the Blind Fiddler laid down his bow, stretched his big arms
out and then rubbed his belly ... We all waited and watched ...

Liam Well, Maggie …

Pat Says he.

Liam Cud fair ate the leg of a donkey.

Pat There was a great hush ——

Everyone hushes

— for we all knowed what was afut ... so with the great hush all eyes
turned on my mother …

Bridie As God is my judge and maker, I haven't a bite to put in the
mouths of none of ye.

Pat Then the tears welled up in her eyes. But Chrissie Hagan who was
with child comes up til her and says, "Never worry yourself Martha
for we can all go over to my place." "No fear," says our big Manus,
"no fear as we will have —— "

John Jo "Bad luck."

Pat "Well," said the fiddler ——

Liam "Well now, I wud like youse all to cast your minds back to the last
lock of hours when not a man nor woman among yis had the mind for
atin' … We'd better play on and that shud put the atin' out of yis ...
Come on, up yis get, them that's dancin', dance, and ye never know
what this new day cud bring."

Pat So we did, even Chrissie Hagan who was with child and m'mammy
who was without grub forgot themselves and threw themselves about
the room to the fiddler's tune.

Dance — a barn dance or folk dance

The morning wasn't full out when suddenly m'Da burst through the
door — with a big sack of potatoes over his shoulder ... He hurled it
intil the middle of the room. "There, get that intil yis — Maggie, lay
on a feast fit for a Blind Fiddler for didn't I get more than I bargained
at the market."

A spot comes up on Pat and the Lights fade on the rest of the stage

Everyone else exits or freezes

But the taties weren't going to last forever, so the next day my father comes up til me and hands me a ten shilling note. "Here, take that son," he says, "and make your way to Belfast and luk for work, for you're not going to make it here." My father was a big quiet sort of a man, not one givin to being soft ... Then I saw what luked like a tear in his eye. "You're a man now, son, so off ye go to the city and make your way there — for there's not what wud keep body and soul together."

The Light fades

Pat exits. (Everyone else does, too, if they have not gone off before)

Black-out

ACT II

The Cave Hill Road house

The pub door is closed and a chair, a Dansette record player, a book and a ruler have been set on the upper level

The Lights come up. A piano can be heard as if Joe is practising off stage; this continues under the following dialogue

Mary enters. She listens to Joe for a minute. She smiles

Mary (*calling*) Kathleen, come up here now, you have to practice.
Kathleen (*off*) I want to do it down here.
Mary No, you will disturb our Joe; he has a piano exam tomorrow.

Mary gets the record player ready during the following

   Kathleen enters

Kathleen Do I have to do this now?
Mary Yes.
Kathleen I'm watchin' *Champion the Wonderhorse.*
Mary Sister Catherine says you have to practice your dancing and your recitations.
Kathleen Stupid oul poems.
Mary They are not stupid ... Now go and stand with your head up and speak nice and loud and clear.
Kathleen (*reluctantly*) There was once an idle fairy.
               His name was Farquar Fly.
               A slothful little fellow he could be.
               Couldn't fly he was so lazy,
               Would languish 'neath a daisy,
               So his fairy fellows wouldn't see.
Mary For God's sake, smile. Sister Catherine says you're not puttin' your heart and soul intil it like the rest of them.
Kathleen It's stupid.
Mary It's not stupid to the rest of the class, just to you ... now do it, next verse.

Kathleen   What is the first line — I forget.

Mary (*looking at the page*) If you meet a fairy fellow and his name is Farkar Fly.

Kathleen   Farquar — not Farkar — you have to speak properly on the Cave Hill Road.

Mary   Don't you dare be so cheeky!

Kathleen   What is the next line?

Mary   Am ... Don't try and diss ... (*having difficulty trying to say dissuade*) diss-u-ad him.

Kathleen (*laughing*) ... dissuade him from his sleep.

Mary   Right, you don't know it ... Learn it for tomorrow. You have my heart broke, wee girl, do you know that? Now, what about the dancin'?

Kathleen   Mammy, I don't want to do this oul dancing.

Mary   You have to practice. Why do you think our Joe is so good? Cos he practices.

Kathleen   You hate me doing this oul dancing; it's only because the nuns said so.

Mary   Everybody else in the school has to do it, so will you.

Kathleen   It's a waste of time practisin' something I am never gonna do.

Mary   Practising — ing ... going — ing ... How many times do I have to drum it into you to use your "ings".

Kathleen   Anyway it's wrong; my daddy says nobody ever danced like this.

Mary   Never mind what your daddy says, Sister Catherine says you will do it. You will do it.

Kathleen   Make our Joe do it ... Why does he not have to do it?

Mary   Don't be ridiculous, he's a boy ... Now, are you ready?

Kathleen   My daddy says his daddy was a great dancer and he was a boy.

Mary   Your daddy says this, your daddy says that, your daddy hasn't to deal with Sister Catherine ... Please, love — please ... I am doing my best for God's sake. Right — ready.

The music is ready. Mary puts the record on and taps out the sevens on a ruler on her hand

Mary   Get ready ... Shoulders back, chest out, stomach in and head held high ... Point your toe, right off we go, and 1,2,3,4,5,6,7 — 1,2,3 — 1,2,3 ...

Kathleen   I can hardly hear it, turn it up.

Mary   No, you will disturb our Joe and I don't want to annoy the neighbours.

Kathleen begins to dance awkwardly, looking at her feet

Mary   (*still tapping*) Keep your hands by your sides and look up and
   not at your feet.
Kathleen   I have to look at them to see what they are doin'.
Mary   Doing — ing. How many times do I have to tell you.

   Joe enters

Joe   (*of Kathleen*) Look at big shipyard feet.
Mary   For God sake.

Kathleen and Joe fight. Mary separates them

Joe   Mammy, will you come and listen to this?
Mary   (*to Kathleen*) You keep practisin' ... I have to hear our Joe.
Kathleen   Practising — ing.

Mary gives Kathleen a look

Joe   Mrs Munroe says I'm going to be playing a Mozart concerto soon.
Kathleen   So.
Mary   Isn't that lovely, son.
Joe   You know he started composing when he was only seven.
Kathleen   What happened to you, banana fingers?
Mary   Well, that Motzart will get a right gonk when he hears you.
   (*Pause*) Don't stop, I want it perfect.

   Mary and Joe exit

Kathleen   Flippin' Cave Hill Road.

*Kathleen starts dancing dutifully, then becomes more abandoned,
dancing wildly round the room*

*Joe's piano-playing can be heard; the sound vies with the music from the
Dansette, making for a cacophony*

*Mary comes in the door and switches off the Dansette. The dance
music stops; the piano continues*

Mary   What the hell do you think you are doing?
Kathleen   Only rakin' about, Mammy, I swear.

Mary You have a bad streak in you, our Kathleen, but I will knock it out of ye.
Kathleen Please Mammy, I don't want to do this ould dancin'.
Mary Dance, or I will murder you — dance.
Kathleen (*in tears*) I want my daddy
Mary Dance, dance, curse you, dance.
Kathleen Daddy — Daddy.

Kathleen dances and cries at the same time. Mary counts maniacally

The Lights go down

Mary and Kathleen exit

The Lights come up again on the pub and the door is opened

Pat is wiping down the benches or the bar counter

Mary enters carrying an envelope. It is clear she hasn't been in the pub for quite a while

Pat is surprised to see her

Mary I need a large sherry.
Pat Mary, what is it? What's up?
Mary We have to do something, Pat — take a look at our Kathleen's school report. (*She hands the envelope to Pat*)
Pat Is that it? Jesus Christ Mary, I thought something was wrong.
Mary Something is wrong.
Pat Some kids is smarter than others — that's no shame.
Mary She can't afford these kinds of marks.
Pat If it's not in the child, it's not in the child.
Mary I thought getting her out of here would be the answer, but her head is always elsewhere, missin' this place, wants to come back — a wee rebel.
Pat Is that so.
Mary I hope you are not going to say I told you so ... It takes time ... I need time.
Pat Maybe she doesn't want what you want for her.
Mary She has no choice, she has to do well.
Pat She is only eleven years of age for God's sake, Mary.
Mary Pat, I had a wee talk with Sister Catherine; she thinks I should send her to board at the Convent.

Pat What?

Mary I think she is right.

Pat A wee talk. You had a wee talk — and that was all it took to for you to decide to send her away.

The hatch opens and Brendan appears

Brendan (*putting his pint glass on the counter*) Another wee bottle there Pat ...

Pat pours Brendan's drink during the following

Jesus, Mary Gormley, I haven't seen you for near on a year. What brings you down among the peasants?

Mary All right, Brendan?

Brendan Not so bad.

Mary How's your John Jo?

Brendan Had to go to England — no work for him here ... It went against my waters. Pat, did you not tell Mary?

Pat Forgot.

Brendan Went for a couple of jobs here but they didn't employ Catholics so I just says, "Son, off ye go ... There is only one thing I ask of ye," says I, "only one thing — don't come back here with an English accent. I don't mind you marrying an English woman, just don't come back talking like her."

Mary Is he working?

Brendan Getting' a wee turn at the building — doing well … And how's the Cave Hill Road and our wee Kathleen — hope she's not talking like all them nobs up there.

Mary Kathleen is fine.

Brendan You'll not break our Kathleen, she's one of us and always will be — a thoroughbred, eh Pat?

Pat (*handing Brendan the drink*) I wanna a word with Mary here before she goes, Brendan, do ya mind?

Brendan Fire away, Pat ... Hey, Mary, don't be givin' him bad ears.

Brendan moves away, closing the hatch himself

Pat Boarding school.

Mary You heard Brendan — what chance has she got if we don't get her an education.

Pat I hardly see her as it is.

Mary She will get home, once a month and school holidays.

Pat She won't know me. I'll lose touch … What did she say?

Mary She doesn't know.

Pat What if she doesn't want to?

Mary Oh, she won't want to, no question about that — but Pat, is she going to thank us in a lot of years' time when she is in some dead-end factory job?

Pat We don't have the means.

Mary If we had said that the first time, we would have got nowhere … If we had given into it the second time, we wouldn't have the Cave Hill Road. I'll make do with less and I have found a job cleaning in an office … It's early in the morning, so I'll be up and out before anybody knows I'm away … You will be there in the mornings for our Joe and I will be back in time to take him to school, so don't you dare tell anybody what I am doing — our secret.

Pat So your mind is made up, no matter what I say.

Mary Pat, don't hate me for this.

Pat I don't hate you, I just feel like a stranger.

Mary Pat, just think how proud you will feel when they are older. Just think how grateful they will be when they have made something of their lives.

Pat looks at her; he can say nothing

Pat I'm thinking of going away for a few days.

Mary What?

Pat Away — for three days.

Mary Where?

Pat On a pilgrimage.

Mary A what? Where?

Pat Lough Derg.

Mary Lough Derg, you in Lough Derg? What in the name a God brought this on?

Pat It's private — between me and God, Mary.

Mary You have never mentioned none a this before; when was the last time you were even in Mass?

Pat Well, maybe it's time I thought about those things.

Mary Are you going to die or something?

Pat No, but I'm going, that's all you need to know.

Mary What about this place?

Pat You can take over.

Mary The day I moved from behind that bar I swore I ——

Pat We'll close then.

Mary Don't be ridiculous — we can't afford to close.

Pat Then we will get your Kevin to take over, he is lookin' a job.

Mary You are going to trust our Kevin with this place.
Pat He's your brother.
Mary Exactly — he has never run a bar.
Pat But he needs a job, he needs to support his family, surely to Christ you understand that, Mary.
Mary All right — but don't you dare tell anybody where you are going or you won't have a Protestant customer left.
Pat All right.
Mary I'll go on then.
Pat Ay … Goodbye Mary.
Mary I'll see you later.
Pat Ay.

Mary exits

The Lights fade to Black-out except for a spot on Pat

The Lough Derg music plays: a song, a capella

Pat produces a fiddle and a fiddle case from behind the bar. He puts the fiddle in the case

The singing stops

During the following voice-over from Kathleen, Pat wraps the case in brown paper, puts on his coat, puts the case inside the coat and exits

A window opens on the image of Kathleen writing a letter and a spot comes up on it

Kathleen (*voice-over*) Dear Daddy, I don't like this school. I miss my friends. Why did you let her send me away? Was I too much trouble? Why don't you write back to me? This is my third letter. There is a school orchestra. A girl in my dorm is playing the classical violin — sounds awful when she practises. I have refused to call it a violin — I call it a fiddle — she says that belittles it ... I thumped her. I won't see you this weekend because you are in that Lough Derg place. A whole weekend is an awful long time to pray, Daddy — you must be very sad about things. Mammy always writes back and tells me all is well with you and our Joe got a place in the academy of music — but I want a letter from you. Tell me about the pub and Bridie and Brendan and John Jo. I miss you. Love Kathleen. P.S. Is old Liam ever going to die?

The Lights fade to Black-out, then come up again on the Lough Derg setting. The pub door and the door over Kathleen's picture are closed

The sounds of the sea, seagulls and an approaching boat can be heard

Adult Kathleen is with the pilgrims — all with their shoes off — at the water's edge; Maggie and Brian are there, with the Old Man seen earlier whose name is Harry. Kathleen is apart from the others, listening to them

"Hail Glorious St Patrick" plays under the following with prayers and rosary-chanting

Pilgrim 1 There she is — land ahoy.

Brian Yes ... That is definitely the cavalry — you can just about see it through the mist.

Maggie Yes ... Yes ... That's her ... Another vessel of lost souls — all heading for the left luggage department.

Old Man Hope one a them lost souls has the futball results.

Brian See you again then next year, Harry.

Old Man God spares me, and my oul chest, you will ... The damp in this place gets to you.

Maggie Sure think of the weight you got off it.

Old Man (*putting his fist to his chest*) In there I'm a young buck again ...

Brian What age?

Old Man Fifteen and ready to kill dead things.

Maggie Weh hey, Harry.

Brian Hey, Harry, you won't get intil the Dockers' club the night — you're under age.

Old Man (*staring out to sea*) I love that first pint after Lough Derg. You sit and you look at it and you know you have every right to have it, you deserve it, you have suffered for it and no man can't take that right away ... I can see it now sittin' there in all its glory and when it goes down it's like nectar.

Maggie Worth the sacrifice, Harry.

Old Man Ay, the bould St Patrick knew what he was doing.

Brian Harry, I don't think he came to this Godforsaken place, holed himself up in a cave for three days just so he could get to enjoy a pint in the Dockers'.

Old Man No ... but he knew that people, now and again, need to sacrifice to appreciate the good things in life ... Here she comes ... (*Shouting out to sea*) Hey, anybody know the score of the Celtic match?

The pilgrims — with the exception of Maggie and Kathleen — exit

Maggie sees that Kathleen is standing watching, without her shoes on

Maggie My time to go now … See ya.
Kathleen I have one more day.
Maggie I hope you find what you're looking for.
Kathleen Thanks, Maggie.
Maggie Enjoy the soup.
Kathleen Actually looking forward to it.

 Maggie exits. Kathleen is left alone

The music fades

The Lights change. Kathleen is now at the icon of Our Lady of Perpetual Succour (one of the rostra)

Kathleen Our Lady of Perpetual Succour ... Did he find the peace he was lookin'? Did you look down on him and tell him we still loved him? We never showed it, because we couldn't show it — none of us — not me our Joe — not even his own wife ... Did he close himself off, or did we shut him out? Did he feel proud of us, like she said he would … That night when we were all last together — what did he feel then?

The Lights fade to Black-out

 Kathleen exits

A rostrum is arranged to represent seats in a concert hall. The window opens on the chandelier

The Lights come up on the concert hall seats and on the chandelier. We hear the sounds of an orchestra tuning up

 Mary and Pat, now older, enter. Pat looks uncomfortable

 A man — Joe's manager — enters with a handful of concert programmes

Manager Mr and Mrs Gormley, over here. Hallo.
Mary Hallo. Pat, he's over here.

Manager My name is Phillip, I'm Joe's manager.
Mary This is my husband Pat.
Manager If you just like to come with me I will show you to your seats.

The Manager shows them to their seats during the following

Kathleen runs on and joins them

Kathleen Sorry I'm late, the traffic was awful.
Mary This is my daughter Kathleen.
Manager Oh, Joe never said he had a sister — very forgetful, these geniuses.
Kathleen Hallo — pleased to meet you.
Manager A pleasure ... These are your seats.
Mary Thank-you.

Kathleen, Mary and Pat sit on the rostrum. They are lit individually. The Manager hands them the programmes

Manager So then, who does he get this wonderful gift from?
Mary I don't know, none of us are musical.
Kathleen Well, actually my father played the fiddle.
Pat Ack sure, I only footered about on it.
Mary Hardly the same thing.
Manager No matter, you must have had a love of it Mr Gormley — I knew it had to be in the family somewhere — and what about yourself, Kathleen?
Kathleen No ... No rhythm at all in me.
Mary Our Kathleen is in the civil service.
Kathleen Not much music there.
Manager Well I am sure you are all very proud of him.
Mary We are.
Manager I better take my seat, it's about to begin. You'll stay behind for the reception?
Kathleen Reception?
Manager Oh, I'm sure Joe just forgot to mention it.
Mary Well, if it is all right.
Manager I can't see any reason why not, you will be most welcome.

The Manager exits

Pat We should check with Joe if it is all right to stay behind.

Mary Oh, Pat, look up at the chandeliers ... I never expected them to be
that big ... Chandeliers — I told him, some day he would be playing in
a room with chandeliers.

The Lights dim. The music starts — a piano solo. They listen

*The Lights fade on all but Pat, listening. We hear what he is imagining:
a fiddle and accordion joining the piano. The piano and Irish music
merge into one. The Lights hold on Pat, then suddenly the music stops
and the Lights go out*

*The Manager enters with three glasses of champagne. He joins
Kathleen and Mary and they take a glass each. Pat stands apart from
them*

The Lights come up again

*Joe enters carrying a glass of champagne. He goes to his father and
hands him the glass. There is an awkward tension between them*

Joe There you go, Dad.
Pat Boys a dear, champagne.
Joe What did you think?
Pat It was good — it was very good.

Pause

Joe I love playing that piece.
Pat It all sounded good.
Joe Good.
Pat Yes — not my music, but I can appreciate …
Joe Oh yeah?
Pat Well … I try.
Joe Needed a fiddle and an accordion, eh?
Pat No ... each man til his own son.

Pause

Joe I have a solo next month with the London Philharmonic.
Pat Good ... very good.

Pause

Joe No, Dad, it's actually not just good, its pretty amazing.
Pat Sorry, son, I am sure it is. I mean …
Joe I'll go phone a taxi for you and Mum … You know what Saturday night is like — might take some time.

Joe exits

Pat is left alone. Kathleen comes over to him

Kathleen On your own?
Pat Our Joe is away to get us a taxi.
Kathleen The reception's only just started.
Joe It's his night … He has his own friends, and I better get back to the pub.
Kathleen Dad. You know you don't have a pub any more.
Pat I know … I know … I just can't get my head round that, our Kathleen. I must have done wrong to deserve all this … I have let everybody down, you, our Joe, your mother, my customers. My customers were all I had left and …
Kathleen Daddy, nobody planted the bomb in the pub because of you, Pat Gormley … it's the times.
Pat All them years of keeping myself to myself and they still show up and tell me to get out — the sons of men I served — good Protestant customers … I have nothing, Kathleen, in this world any more.
Kathleen What brought all this on?
Pat Nothing left, except my pilgrimage … nobody can take that from me … (*To himself*) You should go there some time.
Kathleen Maybe I will.

Everyone exits except Kathleen

The Lights change to the Lough Derg setting

You should go there some time … Well I am here, Da, and I still can't fit you into a place like this … We all grew so far apart. Joe and I have done well. That's all she wanted … maybe that's all you wanted. If it was, why do I feel so empty, why are we so broken up …?

The Lights fade on the Lough Derg setting

Kathleen exits

A coffin is set in the Cave Hill Road setting

> *Mary enters and kneels at one end of the coffin with a rosary. Joe enters and stands as if looking out of a window*

Lights come dimly up on the Cave Hill Road setting

Joe Mum, a couple of men just got out of a car there with a Tyrone reg ... I think they're comin' here.
Mary I can't let them in.
Joe Would my dad still have relatives there?
Mary I can't let them in.
Joe They've got instruments, what time of night do they think it is? Do they think it is a bloody party or something?
Mary Oh, God — they have come to wake him. Please ... Joe ... The noise, the neighbours ...

The doorbell rings

> Send them away, Joe.

Kathleen enters

Kathleen I'll get it.
Mary No, it's a crowd come from the country to wake your daddy.
Kathleen So let them in.
Mary No ... It said in the paper, house private.
Kathleen They have come the whole way from Tyrone, let them in.
Mary No.
Kathleen They want to pay their respects, for God's sake — I'll let them in.
Joe (*stopping Kathleen*) She said no.
Kathleen Mother, you can't.
Joe Don't worry, Mum, I'll sort it.

Joe makes to leave

Kathleen Are you going to deny him the only right he has left?

Joe stops

Joe Deny him, what are you talking about "denying him"? He is dead and she has to live here.

Joe leaves the room

Kathleen It's the custom, the custom where he came from — his home.
Mary He comes from here and it's not our custom.
Kathleen How can you do this? Do you have any feelings?
Mary I want no more said about it.
Kathleen You knew they would come to wake him and you don't even have the decency to give him his last right ... May God forgive you.

Joe enters

Joe Jesus, have you no respect ... It's all right, Mum, they've gone.
Kathleen What respect did she ever give him?
Joe For God's sake — the woman's husband is dead.
Kathleen Yes ... That's it ... That's all he was to you — some woman's husband ... He was your father, remember.
Joe Are you drunk?
Mary Kathleen, that is enough.
Kathleen No, I am going to say what I have wanted to say for a very long time.
Joe I want to mourn my father in peace.
Kathleen Mourn, you'll not mourn him, because you never had any respect for him — he wasn't as clever as you and you made fun of him.
Joe I did what was expected of me.
Mary No brown penny of your fathers was ever wasted on our Joe's education ... You were always one ungrateful child — you got everything you ever wanted from us.
Kathleen No mother, you got everything you ever wanted.
Joe Don't speak to her like that — she has worked her fingers to the bone for us. What is wrong, Kathleen? Is your head still full of how romantic it is to be poor? Would you rather be living in the backstreets?
Kathleen Backstreets ... Did the backstreets not pay for your education and your music? Didn't the gutter pay for the Cave Hill Road? Didn't the money from the backstreets not help put you where you are now?
Joe And what about you? You are no different from me. I don't see you or your kids suffering — and what's that you're driving out there Kathleen, a new BMW ... Oh, you must feel really guilty driving around in that ... Feel bad do you? No, I don't think so ... You are a middle-class Catholic, because she sacrificed to make you that.
Kathleen You are wrong, Joe ... I am not what she made me — I can't be — because if it kills me I will give my children the things that

would have cost her nothing ... All that sacrifice and what is she left with? Loneliness ... She looks out that window, every day ... You don't come and see her, because you have nothing to say to her ... You don't know who she is, you never wanted to ... She doesn't even have a friend or a neighbour she will trust — she was too frightened of who she was.

Mary I never meant to wrong my children.

Kathleen You're right, you never meant to wrong us ... That's what is so sad.

Kathleen exits

Mary Where did I go wrong with our Kathleen? I tried, God help me I tried.

Joe I know you did, Mum, I know.

Mary Will you come and see me more often, son? It's awful quiet up here.

Joe I'll do my best, Mum — it's just the touring — and I'm in demand now in Europe.

Mary You're doing so well, son.

Pause

Well ... Sure ... You'll come when you can ... Your music has to come first ... The main thing is — you never let us down.

Joe I'll have to go ... will you be all right.

Mary Yes ... before you go son ... I something to give you. (*She goes to the bar counter and brings out the fiddle from one of the shelves beneath it*) He wanted you to have it — he said before he died ... I said what about our Kathleen, she was the one that would have wanted that — but for some reason he wanted it to go to you.

Joe Why me?

Mary I don't know why — I am sure he had his reasons.

Joe I can't take it, Mum.

Mary Please, son, it's what he wanted.

Joe holds the fiddle and looks at it. He is very emotional, holding back his tears

Joe Ah, Dad.

The Lights fade to Black-out
  Joe and Mary exit

The Lights come up on the Lough Derg setting

Kathleen I know now why he gave Joe his fiddle. I know why he wanted
me to go on the pilgrimage. You should go there sometime. I think I
know now what he meant. I have one final station.

We hear one verse of "The Hills above Drumquin", played on a fiddle

*The Lights change. One of the doors behind the bar counter is opened,
revealing fewer drinks than previously; we are not in Pat's pub*

  *Manus and Johnny stand at the bar, a Barman behind it. Manus is
  reaching the end of a joke*

Manus So, from that day on they always kept their chickens in the
loft.

They laugh

There is a fierce knock on the upper level door L

Chrissie (*off*) Let me in! Let me in!

The following story is told in the same style as "The Blind Fiddler"

Barman Who is it?
Chrissie It's Chrissie Hagan, let me in …
Barman It's half twelve, we're closed.
Chrissie   It's more than your life is worth to keep me out.
Barman Open up, Manus. Put the latch back on the door.

Manus opens the door

  Chrissie comes into the pub

Chrissie   Strange things is happening out there in Drumquin.
Johnny B'God Chrissie, you're as white as a baker's pinnie, have ya
seen a ghost?
Chrissie   I have … I'll just take a sup and catch m'breath ... I was after

walkin' home. Jamsie McAleer had given me a sup a the poteen — but I swear here and now on my fourteen childers' lives what I am about to tell you is the God's truth. I was walkin home past Seamie the Wheezes' loanin' when I sees this fearsome sight.

Johnny That was Seamie's wife ya seen.

Chrissie I am no mood for coddin' — can't ya see the cut a me w'fright.

Manus Let the woman speak.

Chrissie Thank-you Manus … Any road, I'm walkin' past the loanin' when I hears this sort of a noise. (*She makes a fiddle sound*) And then again. (*She repeats the fiddle sound*)

Johnny 'Twas a sheep, wan a Seamie's sheep.

Chrissie It was no sheep, it was a fiddle.

Barman Are you sure it wasn't a banshee?

Chrissie Have ye ever known a banshee to play the fiddle, you oul fool? I seen it. I seen a ghost playing a fiddle — a fiddle that has played in Drumquin, a fiddle that was never laid to rest. I have just seen Pat Gormley's ghost and well yis may gasp for ye know why he has come back.

Manus Cos she wouldn't let us wake him. He has come back for his wake — Pat has come til Drumquin for to be waked.

There is a knock at the door

Manus I'm not opening the door for it cud be our Pat's ghost.

Barman Open the door.

Knock

Manus Open the door, Johnny.

Johnny You open it, Manus.

Barman Shout out "Who is it?"

Johnny No, you shout "Who is it?"

Chrissie If it is a ghost — he won't answer and then we'll know for once and for all.

Manus Open the door and let in his ghost for it is the custom.

Johnny Who is it?

There are two knocks on the door

The adult Kathleen enters

Kathleen Sorry, I didn't think you'd heard me. Is this McAdoo's pub?

I remember my father talking about this place and I just had to call in … Sorry it's late. My name's Kathleen Gormley.

Chrissie   You a daughter of Pat's.

Manus   You were right Chrissie.

Barman   She's no ghost.

Chrissie   What brings you here, daughter?

Kathleen   I just wanted to see the place he always talked about as a child.

Manus   (*pointing*) See that chair there? That was Pat's.

Chrissie   He sat there and played the fiddle in the fleadh, the music festival, for the last thirty years.

Kathleen   What … no … it's not the same Pat.

Chrissie   Pat Gormley — went til Belfast — Pat Gormley that was not allowed to be waked this very year.

Kathleen   Yes.

Chrissie   Their brother Pat.

Johnny   Every year for the past thirty years, he never missed.

Manus   Once a year for three days every year.

Kathleen   (*as if to Pat's ghost*) You fly oul ghost ... You never went to Lough Derg. You came home …

'The Blind Fiddler' plays under the following, starting as a fiddle solo then developing with the piano, the energy and orchestration building

Listen Da, can you hear it? *The Blind Fiddler of Glenadauch*, can you hear it? And our Joe — can you hear him, can you hear it? You, Da, playing your soul on its journey … Can you hear him, Ma? Dance, everybody — dance for Pat Gormley's soul ... Dance for Pat Gormley's spirit.

Everyone enters and dances a celebratory dance. The door concealing the puppets opens and they dance too

A full-blown celebration develops

THE END

FURNITURE AND PROPERTY LIST

ACT I

On stage: Rostrum that can represent bar counter (with concealed shelf)
Four rostra (two straight, two curved) at seating height arranged in
    boat formation
Behind doors in back wall: drinks and glasses for pub; chandelier;
    church window; dancing puppets; images of **Pat** and **Kathleen**.
    (All doors closed at opening of play)
Doll for **Kathleen** (concealed)

Off stage: Bottle of bleach (Mary)
Whiskey glass (Bridie)
Picnic basket containing picnic including queen cake; rug (Mary)
Bunch of flowers (Kathleen)
Coffin (John Jo, Bridie and Liam)

Personal: Pilgrims: rosaries

During black-out p. 3:

Set: Glasses on bar

During lighting change p.21:

Set: Crate of empty bottles

ACT II

On stage: ON UPPER LEVEL: Chair
Dansette record player
Book
Ruler
ON CONCEALED SHELF OF BAR: Fiddle
Fiddle case
Brown paper

Off stage: Envelope (**Mary**)
Pint glass (**Brendan**)
Concert programmes (**Manager**)
Three glasses of champagne (**Manager**)
Glass of champagne (**Joe**)
Coffin (**Stage Management**)

Furniture and Property List

Personal: **Mary**: rosary

During lighting change p.41:

Strike: Some bottles from shelf behind bar door

LIGHTING PLOT

Practical fittings required:
Various simple interior and exterior settings

ACT I

To open: General exterior lighting suggesting cold and wet conditions

Cue 1	**Old Man**: " ... until God calls me." *Fade lights on pilgrims*	(Page 2)
Cue 2	**Kathleen**: " ...seemed to trouble him — deep down." *Fade lights on* **Kathleen**	(Page 3)
Cue 3	Fiddle plays *Bring up light on picture of* **Pat**	(Page 3)
Cue 4	**Bridie** exits *Change lights to Lough Derg setting*	(Page 8)
Cue 5	**Kathleen**: " ... wasn't it, Da?" *Cross-fade lights to upper level – Kathleen's bedroom*	(Page 8)
Cue 6	**Pat**: " ... beer and whiskey flew and we all felt gay." *Separate area of light comes up*	(Page 9)
Cue 7	**Pat**: "Good-night darling." *Cross-fade lights from bedroom to pub setting*	(Page 10)
Cue 8	**Brendan**: "Eh?" *Fade lights on pub setting*	(Page 15)
Cue 9	Door concealing church window is opened (Page 15) *Bring up light through window*	
Cue 10	**Kathleen**: "...managed to get there at all." *Change lights to outdoor setting*	(Page 17)
Cue 11	**Kathleen**: " ... don't make me tell you, please." *Cross-fade lights to pub setting*	(Page 21)

Cue 12	**Pat**: " … more than I bargained at the market." (Page 24)	
	Bring up spot on **Pat** *and fade on rest of stage*	
Cue 13	**Pat**: " … keep body and soul together."	(Page 25)
	Fade lights	
Cue 14	**Pat** exits	(Page 25)
	Full black-out	

ACT II

To open:	Interior lights on upper level	
Cue 15	**Kathleen** dances; **Mary** counts	(Page 29)
	Fade lights	
Cue 16	**Mary** and **Kathleen** exit	(Page 29)
	Bring up lights on pub	
Cue 17	**Mary** exits	(Page 32)
	Fade lights to black-out except spot on **Pat**	
Cue 18	**Pat** exits	(Page 32)
	Bring up spot on picture of Kathleen	
Cue 19	**Kathleen**: "Is old Liam ever going to die?"	(Page 32)
	Fade to black-out, then bring lights up again on Lough Derg setting	
Cue 20	**Maggie** exits; music fades	(Page 34)
	Cross-fade lights to the icon of Our Lady of Perpetual Succour	
Cue 21	**Kathleen**: " … what did he feel then?"	(Page 34)
	Fade lights to black-out	
Cue 22	Rostrum rearranged; door opened on chandelier	(Page 34)
	Bring up lights on concert hall seats (three separate spots for **Pat**, **Kathleen** *and* **Mary**) *and chandelier*	
Cue 23	**Mary**: " … a room with chandeliers."	(Page 36)
	Dim lights	
Cue 24	Music starts; hold until ready	(Page 36)
	Fade lights on all but **Pat**	

Cue 25	The music stops *Black-out*	(Page 36)
Cue 26	Everyone exits except **Kathleen** *Change to Lough Derg setting*	(Page 37)
Cue 27	**Kathleen**: " … why are we so broken up?" *Fade lights on Lough Derg setting*	(Page 37)
Cue 28	Coffin is set *Bring up dim lights on Cave Hill Road setting*	(Page 38)
Cue 29	**Joe**: "Ah, Dad." *Fade lights to black-oout*	(Page 40)
Cue 30	**Joe** and **Mary** exit *Bring up lights on Lough Derg setting*	(Page 41)
Cue 31	"The Hills above Drumquin" plays *Change lights to pub setting*	(Page 41)

EFFECTS PLOT

All music cues are listed except for those that explicitly call for live music to be played

ACT I

Cue 1	As play begins *Mystical, spiritual music*	(Page 1)
Cue 2	Lights fade *Fiddle music*	(Page 3)
Cue 3	**Bridie** exits *Lough Derg music plays*	(Page 8)
Cue 4	" … beer and whiskey flew and we all felt gay." *Music for Johnny McAdoo song*	(Page 9)
Cue 5	Door concealing church window is opened *Music, singing and praying*	(Page 15)
Cue 6	**Kathleen**: "…managed to get there at all." *Music with piano dominant*	(Page 17)

Cue 7	**John Jo**: "Ay, Maith thu Maith thu."
	*Music for enactment of Blind Fiddler story,
	   including barn dance p.24, after which
	   music ends. (See pp.23-24)*
		(Page 23)

ACT II

Cue 8	As Act II begins *Piano from off stage*	(Page 26)
Cue 9	**Mary** puts record on *Irish dance music*	(Page 27)
Cue 10	Before **Joe**'s entrance *Cut piano music*	(Page 28)
Cue 11	**Kathleen** dances wildly *Piano from off stage*	(Page 28)

Cue 12   **Mary** switches off the Dansette   (Page 28)
            Cut Irish dance music

Cue 13   Lights fade   (Page 32)
            Lough Derg music; a song, a capella

Cue 14   **Pat** puts the fiddle in the case   (Page 32)
            Cut music

Cue 15   Lights come up on Lough Derg setting   (Page 32)
            Sounds of the sea, seagulls and approaching boat

Cue 16   Establish Pilgrims   (Page 33)
            "Hail Glorious Patrick" with prayers
            *   and rosary-chanting; continuous*

Cue 17   Pilgrims exit   (Page 34)
            Fade prayers and chanting

Cue 18   **Maggie** exits   (Page 34)
            Fade music

Cue 19   Lights come up on concert hall   (Page 34)
            Sounds of orchestra tuning up

Cue 20   The Lights dim   (Page 36)
            Piano solo

Cue 21   Lights fade on all but **Pat**   (Page 36)
            Fiddle and accordion join the piano;
            *   the two types of music merge into one*

Cue 22   Lights hold on **Pat**; hold until ready   (Page 36)
            Cut music

Cue 23   **Mary**: The noise, the neighbours ..."   (Page 38)
            Doorbell

Cue 24   **Kathleen**: "I have one final station."   (Page 41)
            Music: "The Hills above Drumquin" played on a fiddle

Cue 25   **Kathleen**: "You came home ..."   (Page 43)
            Music: "The Blind Fiddler", starting as fiddle solo
            *   and developing, the energy and orchestration building*